What Everybody Ought to Know:

28 Facebook Tips

What Everybody Ought to Know:

28 Facebook Tips

Michaela Willlove

2017

First Printing: 2017

ISBN 978-1981425068

Komodo Press
Woodside Ave.
London, UK

Bookstores and wholesalers: Please contact Komodo Press email

zico.pratama@gmail.com.

Trademark Acknowledgments

Ordering Information: Special discounts are available on quantity purchases by corporations, associations, educators, and others. For details, contact the publisher at the above-listed address.

Contents

Introduction

Facebook is an online social networking service. Its name comes from a colloquialism for the directory given to students at some American universities. Facebook was founded on February 4, 2004 by Mark Zuckerberg with his college roommates and fellow Harvard University students Eduardo Saverin, Andrew McCollum, Dustin Moskovitz and Chris Hughes. The founders had initially limited the website's membership to Harvard students, but later expanded it to colleges in the Boston area, the Ivy League, and Stanford University. It gradually added support for students at various other universities before it opened to high-school students, and eventually to anyone aged 13 and over. Facebook now allows anyone who claims to be at least 13 years old to become a registered user of the website. The book is deliberately structured to expand your idea of using the Facebook features. You can take what you are looking for and apply it accordingly. Facebook and most other technologies are best learned by doing, so do not just read this book and do nothing.

This book is published with the title "What Everybody Ought to Know: 28 Facebook Tips". On this issue, we have added some of the latest thought of Facebook with tips for youngster, discuss about fake profile, etc. as well as make improvements layout and cover design to be neater and enjoyable to read.

Hopefully, with the existence of this book, you have a lot of ideas to maximize your communication experience through Facebook.

Write to be understood, speak to be heard, read to grow.

Best wishes!

Michaela

28 Tips and Features in Facebook Not Many People Know

Facebook is extremely keen in displaying an assortment of new components to serve clients. Sadly, there are as yet numerous customers who don't know or don't utilize it properly.

Truth be told, you can use it and make it less demanding from multiple points of view. Among them are to enhance talk understanding, look after security, diminish the utilization of information, and considerably more.

Hence, we have been refreshing the accompanying 28 Facebook components and tips that most likely none you definitely know yet or have not been utilized.

How do I use Facebook properly?

Using Facebook properly means following rules for yourself. Make sure you protect your personal information, identify yourself with things you like and the people you love and keep close to you.

Be who you are. Avoid lying on social media and hide/don't talk negative information about people.

And most of all avoid interacting/finding people who you don't have a deep connection with.

Social networks are now common place deals, promoting, and general business correspondences. Unfortunately, a few people still don't know how to utilize online networking in the work environment without landing in hot water.

Here are the rules, loosely adjusted from IBM's social networking policy with an additional dollop of common sense[1]:

1. DON'T give private or other restrictive data. On the off chance that there's any inquiry in your psyche, fail in favor of keeping quiet.

2. DO identify yourself by name and, when relevant, your role, when you discuss your company or matters relating to it.

3. DON'T write in main individual plural (e.g. "we", "us", "our"). Make it clear you speak for yourself and not on behalf of your firm.

---

[1] 13 Social Media Rules You Should Never Break | Inc.com, https://www.inc.com/geoffrey-james/13-social-media-rules-to-live-by.html

4. DO be careful that whatever you distribute will be open for quite a while, potentially for your whole career.

5. DON'T damage copyright, reasonable utilize, or money related divulgence laws. When you cite some person, connect back to the source if conceivable.

6. DO verify that your online profiles and related content are consistent with how you wish to present yourself to colleagues and clients.

7. DON'T assume that posting namelessly will keep your actual personality mystery if you distribute rude remarks and substance.

8. DO take individual liability for the content that you publish on blogs, wikis, or any other public forum.

9. DON'T overlook that your association's image is spoken to by its kin and what you distribute will definitely consider that brand.

10. DO your best to add value by giving helpful data and point of view instead of mere opinion and bluster.

11. DON'T refer to or allude to the association's customers, accomplices, or providers without their endorsement. Doing as such could land your company in legal trouble.

12. DO show appropriate thought for others' protection and for sensitivities that may exist concerning national issues and religion.

13. DON'T utilize ethnic slurs, personal affront, profanity, or participate in any online lead that would not be satisfactory at work.

How do you underline words on Facebook?

There is a trick you can use, which involves using different Unicode character sets. The following websites let you type your text into a box and then apply the underline formatting you require, then once you have finished, you can just copy and paste the text into your Facebook status or comment box, and away you go: Facebook Status Formatting Tool | Underline text with symbols

Please note the problem with this method is if the device or computer viewing the status does not have the correct fonts installed, the text will not be readable and will just appear as little black boxes.

Yet another method: You could also just create the text with the required formatting in an image editor such as Photoshop or MS Paint etc., then upload your text as a picture.

Is there any way to prevent Facebook friends from inviting you to events?

Snap in the upper right of any Facebook page and pick Settings

Snap Blocking in the left section

In the Block event invites segment, enter the names of companions you would prefer not to get occasion solicitations from. [2]

---

[2] https://www.facebook.com/help/211763458854062/

How do you add your Facebook Fan Page as Your Employer on your personal Facebook profile?

Here's how I did it:

1. Under Personal Profile, click edit

2. Click on Education and Work in left col-
    umn

3. On the new screen, you'll see at the top
    where it's linked you to either a dummy
    page created for your business or nothing at
    all. Click the X out to the right to delete the
    entry. Confirm and delete.

4. Type the name of your Fan Page into the
    search box. If it doesn't come up, click
    "Add Your Company" (where Your Com-

pany" will be replaced with the text you typed in)

5. You must type EXACTLY the name of your Fan Page for this to work.

Your fan page should populate your employer section now.

How do you disable Facebook's "People you may know" feature?

The main reason for this feature is your LOCATION.

"We regularly recommend individuals you may know in light of things you have in like manner, as shared companions, places you've gone by, or the city you live in, or the city you live in," **a Facebook spokesperson said in a statement.** *"But location information by itself doesn't indicate that two people might be friends.* That is the reason area is just a single of the variables

we use to recommend individuals you may know.[3]

Android Users

Those with the Android 6.0 Marshmallow working framework can head into Settings, pick Apps, at that point select Facebook, select Permissions, and afterward set Location to "off."

---

[3] How You Can Deactivate This Creepy Facebook "suggested..., https://www.cbsnews.com/news/how-you-can-deactivate-this-creepy-facebook-feature (accessed August 28, 2017)

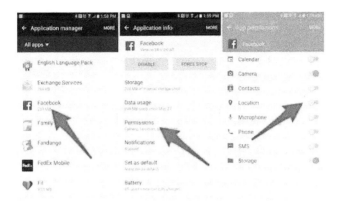

Apple Users

Apple fans who need to maintain a strategic distance from undesirable online networking consideration from outsiders in the area can take after these means. To cripple the component in iOS, make a beeline for Settings, pick Privacy, at that point go to Location Services, and select Facebook. When you choose Facebook, tap on "never" in the rundown of choices for permitting area get to.

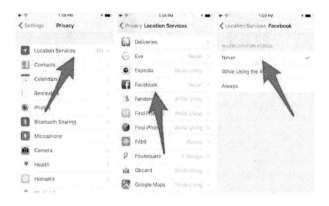

Is there any way to hide the 'sponsored'
posts from Facebook?

No. It's legally required so Facebook will
make sure it always shows.

How do I change the color of fonts on Facebook?

You can't natively change the color of fonts on Facebook. However, Facebook does now let you select background colors for statuses, as shown in the screenshot:

How can I hide my Facebook ID from those people who have my phone number on their contact list?

You can go to setting and change the setting. You can change who can find me using phone number setting.

I believe Facebook is now an endless feed of useless white noise, what can I replace it with?

Curate your feed. It's up to you. Remember that Facebook uses machine learning to attempt to show you relevant content. You can help it learn by giving it signal into what you want to see.

- Use lists. Organize your family into the Family list. Add people who you want to see a lot from into your Close Friends list.
- Follow/unfollow Pages according to your interests.
- Select "See First" for people and pages you actually care about or who post great content consistently.

- Always collapse posts, pages, and ads that you don't want to see or are irrelevant to your interests.
- Unfollow people who you have zero interest in seeing posts from.
- Unfriend people who you don't actually know in any way.

Over a surprisingly short amount of time, you'll see your feed improve dramatically.

How do I see what post my girlfriend likes on Facebook?

"**recent posts liked by Suzy Quzie**" (without the quotes) into the search box at the top of your Facebook page, and it will show you the recent posts liked by her. Obviously, you need to replace that name with the name of your girlfriend. This method utilizes Facebook's "**Graph Search**" functionality which allows you to enter plain English search queries to query Facebook's database. This feature has not been taken off to everybody yet, it's apparently only available to users in the USA or who have their Facebook language set to "**English (US)**," due to stricter privacy laws in the rest of the world.

Is there a service that allows me to search my own Twitter / Facebook posts?

Yes, there is, and it's called Greplin http://www.greplin.com/.

You can search Twitter, Facebook, Linkedin, Dropbox, Gmail, and others. There are a free, premium and a premium plus plan. The services I listed are all in the free program.

Why does the Facebook landing page continue defaulting from "Most Recent" to "Top News"?

I have no inside information or anything, but I believe it has to do with the amount of time since you last logged in—presumably. If you've been gone more than a certain number of hours, you would prefer to see a quick precis of the most popular stories on your feed before you dive back into the most recent minutiae, which may be lacking important events that happened farther back than you are likely to browse.

Why is it important to log out of Facebook?

If you don't log out of Facebook. Facebook will use your Facebook "login cookie" to track your activities across the whole World Wide Web. They can do this because most websites have Facebook Like button widgets on them, so if you visit any website that has a Facebook "Like" widget on it while you are logged into Facebook, Facebook knows exactly who you are and which site you have visited. Facebook can then add that data to the massive amounts of data that they already store about you and sell that information to advertisers.

Another reason to always log out is if someone else accesses your computer and you haven't logged out of Facebook. They will be able to read your private data on Facebook such as messages, etc., and also post as you and contact other people on Facebook as you and change your privacy settings, language settings, "like" inappropriate pages, join inappropriate groups, etc.

How do I disable notifications when someone sends gift request on CityVille?

Open the notifications page, on the information showing Game Request, click on the "x" on the top right of the notification. When you click it, it will ask you whether you want to turn off it or not.Click Turn Off and then these game request notification won't bother you anymore. Problem Solved

I can't view or message my friend in Facebook, why so?

There is a restricted list in Facebook your friend may have somehow mysteriously gotten on this list. Happens all the time with Facebook. Attached is a link to that page. Check it and if she is there remove her.
https://www.Facebook.com/bookmarks/lists

How can you format text (make text bold, italic, underline, etc.) on Facebook posts?

The main way to use text formatting on Facebook is to create a **Facebook Note**, which you can post to your Timeline. The formatting styles you can currently use are as follows:

Bold, *Italic*, **Mono** (text highlighted with a gray background), **Links**, **Lists** (ordered and unordered), **H1** (Heading one), **H2** (Heading 2), **Quotations** and **Code blocks**, you can also insert **Images**.

To create a **Note**

1. If you are publishing as a "Page," Go to your **Page** and click the "**Offer, Event+**" Button above the Status box then Click "**Note.**"

If you are publishing a personal note to

your own Timeline, go to the Notes Page then click the "**Write a Note**" button in the top right corner of the page.

2. Enter your text and to add formatting to some text, highlight the text with the mouse, then the available formatting options (**Bold**, **Italic** or **Mono**) will pop up above the text. For additional formatting options, click the icon with the "4 horizontal lines" () next to your text. This icon allows you to format your text as **H1** (a larger header), **H2** (a medium header), a bulleted list, a numbered list, a quotation, or computer code (H2). You can also click the "image" icon to insert a picture into the note.

Yet another method: You could also just create the text with the required formatting in an image editor such as Photoshop or MS Paint etc., then upload your words as a picture.

Text Formatting in Facebook Messenger (aka Inbox & Chat)

Facebook does allow some basic native text formatting/styling in Messenger. The 4 styles it currently seems to allow is Bold, Italic, "Strike-Through" and "Inline Code". To type text in bold in Messenger, start the text with an asterisk and end it with an asterisk, for example:

This is a test

To type text in italic, launch the text with an underline character and end it with an underline character. For example:

This is a test

To type "strike-through" text, start the text with a tilde character, i.e., "~" and end it with one too. For example:

~~~This is a test~~~

To type text in the "inline code" style, start the text with a ` character and end it with one too. For example

`This is a test`

Facebook will strip the start and end characters and apply either bold, italic or strikethrough formatting depending on which you chose.

Is there a way to get the Facebook page unblocked?

Contact support team and write in your message the detail, saying the 3rd party app caused everything to be posted twice and you shall discontinue the use of that app and that your page is not spam and representing a real thing!

Is there a way to find out the order in which Facebook users "liked" a page I manage?

Yes, there is a way to see the order in which users "liked" your Facebook Page:

1. Go to your Page's **Settings** page, by clicking the "Settings" button at the top right.

2. Click the "**People and Other Pages**" tab, and the individuals who have liked your page will be listed, keep scrolling the page down till it contains all the people who have liked your page.

3. The users who liked your page will be listed in descending order from most recent likers at the top, to most ancient likers at the bottom. Beneath their names will be the date that they "liked" the page.

How might I play out a keyword search on my Facebook Timeline?

One way to search your Timeline is to use the Search Box at the top of your "**Activity Log**" page (https://facebook.com/me/allactivity) enter the text you want to find there, and it will find any posts you made featuring that text.

You can also use the main Facebook search box at the top of any Facebook page, as it is a universal Facebook search, it searches across the whole contents of Facebook including your own and your friend's Timelines.

After you run the search, look through the results. One of the results will have the title **"Posts from Friends and Groups"** and at the bottom of that section, it will have a link to "See

More Posts from Friends and Groups" clicking that will allow you to see more search results (the posts will also include your own posts).

As you wish to search your own Timeline, first put your full Facebook name into the search box, then follow it by the search term you are looking for. For example, if your name was "**Joe Bloggs**" and you wanted to find a post where you mentioned pizza, put the following query into the Facebook search box "**Joe Bloggs Pizza**".

Is it harmful to add a new friend on Facebook without knowing him personally? What could be the possibilities?

I am going to give some scenarios that have happened, as unlikely as they may be. Stuff still happens.

If you're one of those people that post where you're at or when you're going somewhere, a random person that's on your friends could potentially gather enough information about you either from post or pictures or both to actually rob your house while you're gone. This has happened before, many documented times.

He could be a weirdo.

He could be a bot, spam your status with links to crap or virus.

Hell, I could sit here and keep posting the likely bad things some one can do with all of the information that's passed through a person's Facebook, but I don't have all night.

So general rule: Set up your privacy and your friends list, keep new friends on a tighter privacy lock down and only let them see what you want. Until you've grown to trust them, then feel free at your discretion to open the way for them to View whatever you feel is okay.

It's hard to trust random people, just be careful and use common sense. The general rule for not getting screwed over.

How to Get Help Using Facebook?

1."Ask" the Facebook Help Center and find quick solutions.

Enter your question into help search and find your solution from our database of routine inquiries.

On the off chance that you can't investigate your issue with the instructions, they'll provide you with a custom form get in touch with them for additionally bolster.

2.Discuss your problem with the Facebook community.

Search for our discussion to get bolster from other Facebook Facebook users.

3.Contact an engineer if you require help with an application.

Most games and applications you use on Facebook aren't made by Facebook. For support, please submit a form to the developer.

4. Explore our tips and assets.

Look at the Safety Center for information, videos, and resources.

What are some of the best ways of gaining like on your Facebook fan page?

Here are four approaches to get new likes:

1) Tell your friends and family (hard work)
2) Use Facebook ads (complicated interface, $1 each)
3) Buy Facebook likes from an outsider site (infringement of Facebook ToS)
4) Spend $10,000+ every month for a Facebook administration company (impossible for 99%)

To start with, you ought to have an arrangement from the earliest starting point for how you will inspire individuals to like your page and comprehend there are NO QUICK FIXES for becoming your Facebook page. Any arrangement that is great either takes a ton of work or a considerable measure of cash. There are a large number of Facebook pages attempting to motivate individuals to like them that offer extraordinary substance, influence people to giggle, and do the majority of the other right things. The truth of the matter is that individuals' consideration on Facebook is profoundly aggressive and seeking after the best while making a page is no superior to doing likewise in some other piece of life. Manufacture it, and they won't specifically come unless you have set up a solid following in different ranges as of now. For instance, make the iPhone 6 and reveal to them a discharge date and they will come! Construct the 501st Facebook page about Barack Obama or your new business, and they more than likely won't come.

Therefore, begin with an arrangement for how you will get individuals to your page. It is possible that he has moves you will make yourself or that another person will improve the situation you. You could choose to setup a Facebook publicizing effort all alone, tell your loved ones using a Facebook message took after by a welcome, and email your associates on LinkedIn. 9 times out of 10, an arrangement like this will fulfill a couple of preferences and nothing more. Many individuals are content with these outcomes and want to impart to a couple of companions as opposed to offering to people they don't have the foggiest idea. Given that you likely hunt down these terms and are perusing this to figure out how to improve the situation than this, there are more approaches to get more individuals on your page.

Another course is to find an associate that can empower you to get a more noteworthy measure of the perfect people to like your page. This could be anything from getting a sidekick to post your page on their page and welcome their colleagues to get your own particular TV advancements like one page did here in the US. In picking an accessory, you have to settle on your objectives ahead of time.

In case you are going for great inclinations from interested people that will like your posts, shop at your store, and buy your things, offering something of noteworthy worth, for instance, time, essentialness, or feedback on other developed Facebook pages might be your best course. In works like this, you would extend your chances to get people that you unquestionably know are possessed with similar pages to take a gander at yours. This is a high gauge and strong obligation approach that puts aside an important measure of a chance to do precisely. These methods are frequently adequately used by young people that have a broad measure of convenient time and are significantly unique using online systems administration media. Everything considered, business specialists with livelihoods and working mothers have furthermore associated these frameworks with advance. In this way, this approach frequently is not ideal for people that are in the penchant for consuming through money to build up their effect or that have a limited measure of time.

Have cash to spend and additionally are short on time and need to become your new Facebook page without running the tiresome gauntlet of physically getting the greater part of your new likes? There are mechanized frameworks and brilliant organizations that can help with that.

In outline, there are several approaches to get new likes:

1) Work hard by explaining to every one of your loved ones WHY they should like your page. To think about a decent

pitch, envision what somebody would need to state to you to motivate you to like their page.

2) Pay $10,000+ per month to manage your page. This probably isn't an option for most but if you can afford it, go for it!

3) Violate the Facebook ToS by acquiring counterfeit profiles and "genuine fans" from administrations that have "systems" that are really phony profiles. Much great organization and little pages alike have utilized this technique. All things considered, it is not a smart thought.

4) Run your own Facebook advertisements or get with an organization that can do it for you. This is the most ideal approach to develop your page on a financial plan.

How can you detect a fake profile on Facebook?

Here is a list of 10 methods to identify a fake Facebook account.

1. Look for photos in the profile. If there is only one picture of the individual in the whole profile, it makes it very obvious that the record is phony.

2. Check out remarks, divider posts, and comments. On the off chance that the customer hasn't invigorated a status for significantly long time and hasn't been related to any divider posting or commenting on different states, it infers that the profile is presumably going to be fake.

3. Take a gander at the current activities.If it is that the client has quite recently been including randomers and making new

companions and that there are no pages preferred or bunches went along with, it proposes that the client is controlled by directly including individuals and subsequently the profile is fake.

4. Look at the companion list.If found that most extreme of the companions is the inverse sexual orientation, it can be accepted that the profile is utilized either for no particular reason or for easygoing dating.

5. Look for the info. I found that there are no perfect connections given concerning class or training organizations or working environment and that the client is searching for dating and inspired by the two men and ladies, it hints at phoniness.

6. Check the birth date. Birth dates like 1/1/XX.....or......31/12/XX are standard between counterfeit records as it is very exceptional and straightforward to sort in.

7. Fake profiles of girls usually have a contact no. for their info. Let's be honest, young ladies barely will have their contact no. in public. So look out if the client uncovered information that is impossible for global clients to disclose out in the open.

8. Look out for recent wall posts, if u see loads of people asking...'THANKS FOR THE ADD....DO I KNOW YOU'......and yet the post stays unanswered... It will undoubtedly be a fake one.

9. Look for common traits used on Facebook, like.Using applications such as Farmville, pet society, etc....and adding siblings. If these characters are not found by the user, the profile is highly inactive or fake.This point can't single handily prove the fakeness. However, this will be a supporting clue along with other points.

10. If you are quite confident about the profile's fakeness and want to be absolutely sure, try browsing google for some random profile pictures. Fake profile pictures are generally chosen from google and keeping in mind that perusing through it, you should happen upon the photo the client decided for the fake record.

Facebook tips for someone young?

Set your profile to private so only your friends can see it. Do this by going into the security settings tab on the top right of the Facebook toolbar.

Just don't add people you don't know and keep your profile private and you will be okay. Just set it so that only your REAL friends can access it and don't become one of those people who add everyone they can to win some stupid popularity contest. And don't ever give your password to anyone.

Debate on Facebook Tips

Invasion of privacy, like when you apply for a high pay job employees look for your name on Facebook and can tell if you are serious about the job; or not even before the interview in person; cyber bullying by having too many Facebook friends over 80% them could be those you don't know and never met!

Facebook is going to go in stock, and you will be worth 120 dollars per share! And what do you get nothing? Absolutely Nothing and a whole bunch of invasion of privacy!

If a friend suggestion appears on Facebook with no mutual friends or any connection, does it mean they are looking at my profile?

That may be the case sometimes, but from my experience, Facebook is actually much more insidious. From my personal experience, a lot of these suggested friends turned out to be people that work/are friends with one of my parents, who do not have Facebook, and with whom I have no other connection whatsoever.

I hypothesize that Facebook has algorithms which analyze the network of people and can sometimes detect possible missing nodes in the network of individuals. When such a node is found, they only take the friends it would have, and then suggests those 2nd-degree people to you.

To give my hypothesis more stable groups, I also discussed it with my (now ex) university professor (who is specialized in machine learning) who agreed it is more than plausible.

Can people see when I visited their Facebook page?

No, Facebook doesn't give individuals a chance to track who views their profile. Third-party apps also can't provide this functionality.

If you run an application that cases to offer this capability, please report the application.

What are the top reasons to avoid Facebook?

Here are my top 5 reasons to avoid Facebook:

1) **It stimulates procrastination** - this kind of social media keep me from my work as I want to check each message I receive immediately which disturbs my work flow. I tried to put my phone on silent, but that didn't work for me. As for avoiding wasting time on these sites while working on the computer, there are apps to block social media sites for a certain amount of time like StayFocusd, SelfControl or LeechBlock.

2) **It's addictive** - I noticed I tend to spend way more time on it than I want to, as I keep scrolling as some form of FoMO.

A report from the Royal Society for Public Health even described social media in general as more addictive than cigarettes and alcohol.

3) **It's a waste of time** - The majority of the posts I come across are actually not worth reading. First of all, a lot of people post things without putting a good thought into it which can result in sharing articles based on pseudo science or bluntly sharing their opinion without putting the effort in getting to know the different sides of a story. Secondly, I think a lot of posts are shared with the wrong intention. Examples would be people sharing selfies to get attention as the primary motivator or sharing posts with the intent to shame others.

4) **It shows an unrealistic world** - Most people show one side of their day-to-

day life resulting in a ridiculous positive (filtered) picture. It can make other people feel inadequate about their own life. Some studies even link social media use to increased rates of depression, see here, here and here.

5) **It's superficial** - I used to follow some science and/or news pages, but I found that most of these posts/ shared articles are written in such a way that they appeal to a big audience. This means short texts, not going deep into the subject, some of these so called scientific pages even post articles that aren't properly fact checked, and if you learn anything from it, it's passive learning as you aren't going to use most of this information in real life anyway.

All in all, life is short. Being on Facebook costs precious time, I rather spend on going out into the world, learning- and doing things I genuinely find interesting.

Index

Other Books By Kanzul Ilmi

	**Excel Functions and Formulas Pocketbook**
	Ali Akbar; Zico Pratama Putra
	Geared toward the intermediate to advanced Excel 2016 user, this pocketbook provides explanations and context for many powerful Excel 2016 spreadsheet formulas and functions. Step-by-step instructions for many formula/function-related features such as using range names, and Excel's troubleshooting features.
	**Visual Basic.NET All Versions**
	Ali Akbar; Zico Pratama Putra
	Visual Basic .NET is a radically new version of Microsoft Visual Basic, the worlds most widely used rapid application development (RAD) package. Whether you are just be-

	ginning application development with Visual Basic .NET or are already deep in code, you will appreciate just how easy and valuable the VB.NET Language Pocket Reference is.
	**Mastering 37 WhatsApp Tricks**
	Zico Pratama Putra
	Here's what you'll learn: - How to make WhatsApp account without a phone number - How to add robot like bot in telegram & schedule your automatic message - Knowing someone location through WhatsApp - How to backup WhatsApp message to cloud storage - The secret to edit photos ala snapchat before send

	- Make your WhatsApp friend damage (crash) and unused, etc.
	**Autocad 2016 from Zero to Hero**
	Ali Akbar; Zico Pratama Putra
	The objective of this book is to provide you with extensive knowledge of AutoCAD, whether you are taking an instructor-led course or learning on your own. AutoCAD 2016 From Zero to Hero is an ideal reference guide, unlike tutorial-oriented books where specific information is hard to found. This book helps you become an AutoCAD expert and has been fully updated to cover all of AutoCAD's new capabilities.
	**Windows Troubleshooting Tips**

	for Daily Usage
	Ali Akbar; Zico Pratama Putra
	Learn how to troubleshoot Windows the way the experts do, whatever device or form-factor you're using. Focus on the problems that most commonly plague PC users and fix each one with a step-by-step approach that helps you understand the cause, the solution, and the tools required.
	**Two in One : Excel and Access 2016 for Beginners**
	Ali Akbar; Zico Pratama Putra
	Microsoft Excel and Access are two most important software in MS Office package. Microsoft Excel is used for spreadsheet analysis and Access is used for some relational database data operation. This two software are mandatory to help any of your office needs. This Two in One Excel and Access 2016 book

	is very, very different to any other computer book you have ever read.

About the Author

 Michaela Willlove, M.Sc. is an active engineering practitioner and a computer science book writer. A lot can be assumed when you first see Michaela, but at the very least you'll find out she's good-natured and intelligent. Of course, she's also trusting, respectful and idealistic, but they're far less prominent, especially compared to impulses of being monstrous as well.

Her good nature though, this is what she's pretty much known for. There are many times when friends count on this and her sensitive nature whenever they need help.

Nobody's perfect of course and Michaela has less pleasant traits too. Her disloyalty and negativity aren't exactly fun to deal with on often personal levels.

Fortunately, her intelligence shines brighter on most days. She continued his PhD at the Queen Mary University of London in Human Computer Interaction field. She writes and speaks at various events in Germany & UK.

Can I Ask a Favour?

If you enjoyed this book, found it useful or otherwise then I'd really appreciate it if you would post a short review on Amazon. I do read all the reviews personally so that I can continually write what people are wanting.

If you'd like to leave a review, then please visit our Amazon book link.

https://www.amazon.com/dp/B0756MT6V5

Thanks for your support!